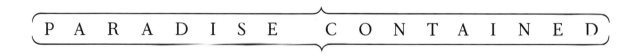

PARADISE CONTAINED

Paradise

CONTAINED

Growing and Decorating with Flower Bulbs

WILLIAM STITES
Photography

KATHRYN GEORGE
Styling

MARY SEARS
Text

DOUBLEDAY
New York London Toronto Sydney Auckland

P U B L I S H E D   B Y
D O U B L E D A Y

a division of Bantam Doubleday Dell Publishing Group, Inc. ~ 666 Fifth
Avenue, New York, New York 10103 ~ DOUBLEDAY and the portrayal of
an anchor with a dolphin are trademarks of Doubleday, a division of
Bantam Doubleday Dell Publishing Group, Inc.
Library of Congress Cataloging-in-Publication Data

Stites, William
     Paradise contained / William Stites, ~ 1st ed.
        p.   cm.
     ISBN 0-385-41195-2
     1. Bulbs.   2. House plants.   3. Container gardening.   4. Forcing
(Plants).   I. Title.
SB425.S75   1990
635.9'86 ~ dc20   90-31232
                                                          CIP

Copyright © 1990 Smallwood and Stewart ~ All Rights Reserved ~
Designed by Patricia Kovic ~ Printed in Singapore ~ November 1990
First Edition ~ Produced by Smallwood and Stewart, Inc. ~ New York City

CONTENTS

INTRODUCTION

9

CHAPTER I

Cultivating Pleasures

13

CHAPTER II

Hardy Bulbs

39

CHAPTER III

Tender Bulbs

67

GARDENER'S RESOURCES

91

ACKNOWLEDGMENTS

96

ULBS ARE AMONG the most versatile and adaptable of flowers, providing a crowning touch to a garden in any style. These glorious flowers are at home anywhere, taking their place in woodlands or meadows, in rock gardens, in precise formal plantings, or in jumbled cottage gardens. During the early months of the year, bulbs are the heroes of the garden, coming into bloom early on, when most herbaceous plants are barely visible above the soil, and brightening the garden with vibrant bursts of color. ℂ Growing bulbs in containers allows many urban dwellers and others who do not have garden space to truly live with flowers, and one exciting and satisfying way to enjoy bulbs indoors is by forcing ~ or coaxing ~ them to bloom out of season. When all outdoors is held in a gray dormancy, forced flowers cannot help but remind us of warmer months and bring a sense of the imminent renewal of spring. Bulbs complement any room's furnishings ‑‑ from rustic to formal ~ and open endless possibilities for home decoration. A crate packed with chrome-yellow daffodils in bloom on a side table brings a room to life in midwinter, with a vibrancy and an energy that few arrangements of cut flowers can approach. Once the simple principles of forcing have been mastered, there is an enormous range of bulbs that can add their colors and fragrance to a room ~ more than enough to keep the flower-lover enthralled during the otherwise bleak winter months. ℂ In the following pages, we explain not only how to coax bulbs into bloom in winter ~ ahead of their natural growing season ~ but also how to grow some bulbs indoors successfully during the other months of the year. You will learn how to select and plant bulbs, how to choose and use containers, and above all, how to get the best results from a wide range of flowering plants. ℂ *Paradise Contained* describes and shows dozens of flowers in almost every shape, size, and color. Some of these~tulips, narcissi, and hyacinths, for example~are what botanists call "true bulbs." A true bulb actually contains an embryonic flower, a stem, and leaves, all surrounded by fleshy layers of stored-up food. Other plants have a somewhat similar storage method, but differ in various ways botanically. These bulb-like plants are often referred to as "bulbs" by most gardeners and include corms, rhizomes, tuberous roots, and tubers. Some well-known plants in these categories are crocus {corm}, bearded iris {rhizome}, dahlia {tuberous root}, and cyclamen {tuber}. ⅭⅬ Gardeners who enjoy growing bulbs outdoors will take equal~if not greater~delight in using bulbs not only to provide decorative accents, but also to bring color, fragrance, and cheer to the home year-round.

CHAPTER I

THE COLORFUL FAMILY of plants known as bulbs are justly popular. They are relatively easy to grow, and range from tender tropical varieties to hardy flowers that are found on snow-covered mountain slopes. In size they will vary from miniature varieties just a few inches in height to tall, imposing plants.

Daffodils, like many hardy bulbs, are happier in the slightly moist climate of a bathroom. In this starkly monochromatic bathroom, their intense color gives them far greater prominence.

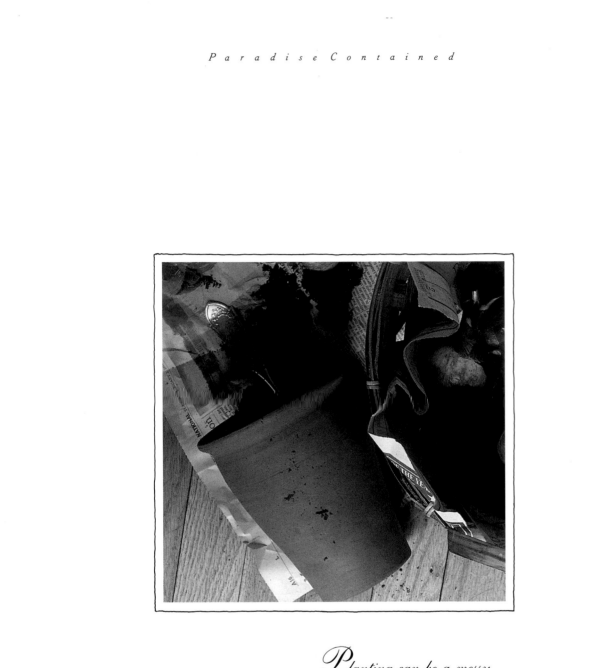

$\mathscr{P}$*lanting can be a messy*
business; newspaper protects tables and floors from
potting mix, bits of vermiculite, and water spills.

For the purposes of this book, we refer to any plant that stores all its energy for blooming within an underground storage organ as a bulb. Unlike seeds, which need soil for sustenance, bulbs carry within their fleshy form all the food necessary to take them through the period of dormancy that is vital for growth and bloom. Tulips, narcissi, and hyacinths, for example, are what botanists call true bulbs. If you were to split one of these bulbs in half, you would see the leaves cradling a baby bud. Sometimes this bud will actually look like a little flower. Around the bud are white meaty scales, which are all the "groceries" the bulb requires. The basal plate at the bottom of the bulb holds the scales, along with the flower stalk and roots. The entire bulb is dressed in a thin outer skin called a tunic. True bulbs are generally the easiest to force into bloom out-of-season. Strictly speaking, many of the plants described here differ in their food-storage organs and are not true bulbs. They store all their food within themselves just as true bulbs do,

Flower bulbs have a real affinity for of baskets, above, perhaps deriving from their common roots in nature.

Just a couple of weeks away from blooming, hyacinths, below, develop rapidly. At this stage, their asparagus-like heads have begun to rise.

but are classified as corms, rhizomes, tuberous roots, or tubers. Crocuses and freesias, for example, are really corms~short underground stem bases swollen with food. Dahlias and ranunculus are actually tuberous roots~enlarged stem tissues easily distinguished from bulbs and corms. Lilies of the valley are rhizomes; cyclamen, clivia, and all anemones are tubers, which have no protective tunics and take on a variety of shapes.

BULB TYPES

For the purposes of this book we have divided bulbs into two basic groups: "hardy" and "tender." Hardy bulbs are those that can withstand freezing temperatures and would normally be planted outdoors in the fall to bloom the following spring. Daffodils, tulips, hyacinths, grape-hyacinths, crocuses, dwarf irises, and colchicum are hardy bulbs. Tender bulbs do not survive below zero temperatures and in colder regions are planted in the spring to bloom during the summer months. Amaryllis, gloxinia, and freesia are tender bulbs.

Hardy bulbs usually bloom four to five months after planting, and would normally be planted mid-fall to late fall.

Forcing hardy bulbs, however, compresses this period, and they can be brought to bloom in midwinter. Hardy bulbs must be planted in soil and usually need a cooling period of several weeks in temperatures of 40° to 50°F before they will bloom.

Some bulbs, such as hyacinths, can be forced into bloom quite easily and certain cultivars of others such as crocuses, grape-hyacinths, tulips, and dwarf irises need a little more care. Many more cultivars can be forced when one has access to the controlled growing conditions of a greenhouse.

Tender bulbs can also be forced, but not through the same cooling methods. The easiest and most popular tender bulbs to force are those with the greatest stores of food~the large amaryllis and 'Paper-white' narcissus bulbs, for example.

SELECTING AND STORING BULBS

It's possible to have plants in bloom indoors all year-round if you choose your bulbs carefully. Bulbs are generally sold at planting time, so for hardy bulbs, make a trip to the local garden center or nursery in late summer or early fall. Or leaf

*At the end of a hallway,
lemon-yellow 'Bellona' tulips nest in a
nineteenth-century painted basket on a New
England twig table.*

*A simple terra-cotta pot
of miniature 'Tête-à-Tête' daffodils is a good foil
for a collection of gilded curtain rod finials.*

through the catalogs of mail-order suppliers that specialize in bulbs that will begin arriving about that time. A glance around the marketplace, whether nursery or catalog, will introduce you to the wide variety of flowers that you can grow. Tender bulbs are generally available in the spring, but this can vary and you may locate a year-round source.

The earlier you shop, the better the selection will be. Buy your bulbs or place an order by mail as soon as the bulbs become available. Mail-order sources generally carry more unusual bulbs and can offer more of a selection than most garden centers. For forcing, choose bulbs marked appropriately or ask your nursery for advice.

If you're buying bulbs {true bulbs, rhizomes, tubers, tuberous roots, or corms} in person, choose large, firm, healthy-looking ones. Avoid lightweight bulbs {they have probably dried up} or soft, mushy bulbs {they are rotten}; hold the bulbs in your hands to feel the relative differences between each. Don't buy bulbs that are already sprouting. Most likely, they've been prematurely exposed to warm conditions and have not yet developed the necessary roots to produce spectacular blossoms. Discard any bulbs that show signs of extensive disease or insect infestation～meaning that fifty percent or more of the bulb is affected.

Your bulbs are alive, though the papery brown skins common to true bulbs and bulb-like structures may fool you into thinking otherwise. Treat them as if they were eggs about to hatch: don't drop them, and protect them from extreme temperatures. Bulbs purchased in late summer or fall for forcing are in dormancy, the first of four stages a bulb goes through in order to bloom. The other three are root development, sprout development, and, finally, blooming.

Plant your hardy bulbs as soon as you get them. If this isn't possible, a cool dark place～such as an unheated room, a garage, basement, or porch with temperatures ranging between 45° to 50°F {but never warmer than 63°F}～is suitable as storage for several weeks. Keep the bulbs well-ventilated to prevent them from rotting during storage; open the paper bags they come in, or store them in mesh bags, or spread the bulbs on open trays so that air can circulate around them.

If necessary, you can store bulbs in the refrigerator. Keep them away from ripe fruits and vegetables, which give off a gas that's harmful to the bulbs. A spare refrigerator in the basement would be a perfect place to store bulbs. If you plan to force the bulbs, this storage period must be counted into the recommended cooling time. It's very important to be aware that some bulbs are poisonous ~ daffodils, colchicum, and lily of the valley, for example ~ so households with young children should keep bulbs out of the kitchen refrigerator, where they might be mistaken for food.

CHOOSING A CONTAINER

Bulbs can be planted in any number of containers, depending on the kind of effect you want to achieve. Traditionally, bulbs were forced in clay pots or in glass or china bowls. But many conventional containers are being discarded in favor of more informal ones. Nowadays, the kitchen is being raided for its soup tureens, vegetable serving dishes, glass carafes, and old canisters. The chips and cracks in a favorite piece of china or pottery may disqualify it from everyday use but render it perfect as a container for flowering bulbs.

A collection of old coffee-cups can be filled with tiny crocuses or grape-hyacinths, or an old stoneware jug with a single stately amaryllis. Those containers that can't serve as planters because they are too big or don't have drainage holes can be used as cachepots,

disguising the functional plastic flower-pots that actually hold the bulbs.

A quick tour through your kitchen, attic, garage, basement, or even a child's playroom will yield all sorts of containers that would make suitable homes for fledgling bulbs. The yard sale, basement, or garage can be a virtual treasure chest, offering up old wooden drawers, decorative tin cans, weathered wooden boxes, even brightly painted children's pails. Wooden flats, fruit boxes, and wine cases are spacious enough for more generous displays of bulbs, so even a large planting of tulips won't seem overcrowded. The unfinished wood's rustic look can be further enhanced by covering the soil with sphagnum moss or sprinkling it with any type of fast-growing grass seed.

Still, the clay, or terra-cotta, pot remains the most traditional and practical container for any plant. It has the advantage of "breathing" with the plant and letting water evaporate through its porous surfaces naturally. {Of course, this does mean that you have to water your plant more often.} A clay pot looks appropriate in any setting, and has a suitably dignified appearance.

A six- to eight-inch pot is a popular size for forcing bulbs, and can generally hold three hyacinths, six daffodils or tu-

The drama of
flower bulbs~the first plucky shoots, the baby buds,
the luscious blooms~is a source of continuing
fascination. Here a flat of white tulips ebbing
from their peak assumes a poignant air.

*Tulips should spend the
waning days of their bloom in a cool area.*

lips, or fifteen crocuses. The pot you use should be no less than four inches in depth. {The depth tends to increase with the diameter of the pot.} A pot should be only slightly greater in diameter than the bulb or bulbs you put in it, since crowding encourages vigorous root growth. For several larger bulbs, such as top size daffodils, make sure your pot is at least eight inches around.

PLANTING MEDIUMS

You can force your bulbs in soil, water, or gravel, depending on the bulbs you've chosen. The planting medium does not provide food for the bulbs {they already hold sufficient nutrients} but will act as an anchor for the developing roots and will hold the important moisture the bulb requires in order to grow.

Regular soil tends to dry out too quickly and compact, restricting root growth. Equal parts loamy soil, peat, and sand make a fine planting mixture, or simply choose a good-quality, soilless potting mixture from your garden center. Good drainage is key; you don't want your bulbs to rot.

Certain bulbs can be grown in water. This is called hydroponic forcing. Crocuses, hyacinths, and 'Jingle Bells' tulips are popular choices. Hourglass-shaped glass containers suspend the bulb just above the water line, allowing the roots to grow downward to gather water while preventing the bulb from sitting in the water and rotting. Pretty glass jars of the proper shape can also be used. A chunk of activated charcoal keeps the water free of algae, for a clear view of the developing roots.

The planting medium you choose affects the future viability of the bulb. Bulbs forced in water deplete all their nutrients in the blooming process, and must be discarded afterwards, but bulbs forced in soil can be transplanted to the garden at a time of year when the soil is workable, but it may take them a year or two to recoup their strength and bloom normally again.

Serene amidst the creative energy in Sara Stites' Connecticut studio, a flat of lilies of the valley thrives in the north light.

25

*Unfinished-wood flats
are versatile planters, equally hospitable to
'Barrett Browning' narcissus, grape-hyacinth,
and lily of the valley. These flats were sprinkled
with fast-growing grass seed.*

The key is to start early. Bulbs can stay in cold treatment as long as you like; the roots just keep developing. The longer the bulbs are held in the cold, the taller your flowers will be. If you spot a long-stemmed beauty, chances are it was cooled longer than suggested. Generally, bulbs cooled less than recommended result in smaller plants, and take longer to force into bloom.

Wherever you store them, water your bulbs thoroughly beforehand, and keep the soil moist throughout the cooling period. You're growing roots here, and you don't want your bulbs to dry out.

By far the best way to create the cool, 40° to 50°F conditions required for forcing is to hold the potted bulbs in an old refrigerator for the weeks they need to develop their roots. In fact, for many apartment dwellers and for southern gardeners in regions where temperatures do not fall below freezing, refrigeration may be the only way they can grow hardy bulbs. With this accurate control of the temperature, you should have a high success rate. Alternatively, choose a spot in an unheated basement or garage where temperatures do not fall below freezing, and keep your pots there for the cooling period.

Digging an outdoor trench for your potted bulbs is a traditional but more laborious alternative for cooling. Dig the trench below the frost line on a sloping patch of land, so water drains away easily. A layer of sand, cinders, or gravel on the bottom of the trench will ensure additional drainage, especially if the trench will be exposed to winter rains.

Place well-watered pots of bulbs in the trench. Surround pots with about two inches of vermiculite, peat moss, or some other soft, insulating material. Water them until the first frost. Then cover the pots with a further insulating "blanket" of hay, pine boughs, peat moss, or fir bark. This will prevent the bulbs from freezing even when the ground temperature falls below zero.

Extra long labeling sticks will come in handy here, when you're reaching into a deep trench trying to locate which pot to extract and bring indoors.

FORCING HARDY BULBS

The forcing process for hardy bulbs is fairly straightforward and is possible for an amateur to master. All you need are some simple materials, and a way of monitoring the temperature of the bulbs. Most importantly, set up a timetable for cooling the bulbs in darkness {if required}. First, choose your bulbs, an appropriate container, and the proper planting medium. Then get out your calendar or a special gardening journal you've prepared just for this purpose. Plot your planting times. The fun part is bringing the plants out into the light and warmth and watching the flowers appear ahead of schedule.

Showy flowers are the reason for forcing bulbs. But first the roots must have time to develop so that they can support top growth. Spindly or short stems, no flowers and all leaves, are the result of insufficient root growth. Give your bulbs the recommended time~which varies from bulb to bulb~they need to develop healthy roots and the cool, dark conditions, about 40° to 50°F.

POTTING BULBS

The best time to pot bulbs is as soon as you have purchased them or received your order. Generally speaking, plant the bulbs a half inch to an inch below the soil, so their tips are just visible. Exceptions include amaryllis, clivia, and other tender bulbs, whose top third should be left exposed. Bulbs enjoy being crowded when forced, so space them only about an inch apart, but do not push them into the soil. Rather, fill the container about halfway with soil, add the bulbs, and fill in the soil around them.

Each pot should be clean, with either a drainage hole or a one-inch layer of gravel in the bottom. Scrub and rinse pots that have been previously used. Soak clay pots overnight so they won't absorb moisture from the planting medium when you pot your bulbs. Be sure to provide gravel for drainage in unusual pots without drainage holes.

When you pot bulbs for forced flowers that will be subjected to a cooling period, be sure to label them with the names of the bulbs planted in them, as well as the dates they were potted.

A PLANTING JOURNAL

A special gardening journal is useful for noting the planting time of each pot of bulbs you are forcing. With each bulb requiring a different kind of care, it's a little like juggling several balls in the air at once. But the results make the effort worthwhile. Some gardeners prefer making notations on their regular appointment calendar so that they don't miss an important date for planting or for moving the bulbs out into the light.

Unlike flowers outdoors,
these crimson 'Bing Crosby' tulips can be enjoyed
long after dusk. Set into a corner of the stair
landing, one of the most heavily trafficked areas
of the house, the tulips beguile the passerby.

Whatever your method, the only time for planting hardy bulbs for forcing is between October 1 and November 15. Generally, bulbs planted early will bloom first, and late plantings will produce late flowers, but quite often the same variety, planted even a couple of weeks apart, will bloom at almost exactly the same time. This will not hold true for two different varieties, even if they are closely related and in the same genus.

When your journal or calendar shows that the correct cooling period has passed, it's time to bring your first pots indoors. Mats of roots will have formed below the soil surface and the tops of the plants will show signs of growth. Sprout development begins now, the last stage before blooming. Bulbs potted on October 1 come inside around January 1, and so on. If you want to have plants blooming all winter long~and who can resist this possibility?~bring a few pots into the warmth of the house every week.

You'll need to vary the temperature of the room and the amount of sunlight the bulbs receive once they have been brought indoors, depending on where they are in the growth cycle. Bulbs that have just come in from the cold need a drink. Setting the pots in a pan of water allows the bulbs to absorb the moisture they need. For the next week or so, keep them in half-light at about 50°F. Remember, they have just come in from a cold, dark environment and can be shocked by the sudden change. Setting them under a table or bench in a cool room is ideal.

Once the bulbs are a bit more acclimated, the combination of a very cool room and full sunshine will best simulate spring and promote development, if shoots have not already appeared. A room that never gets warmer than 50° or 60°F at night is ideal. If you can keep temperatures low at his stage, you'll be rewarded with stronger, healthier flowers in three or four weeks.

Once the flowers start to open, move the pots out of direct sunlight. At night, the flowers can tolerate a room as cool as 40°F. Like a florist's refrigerator, this makes the flowers last longer.

Keep your bulbs moist. The bulb's

*The versatile hyacinth,
here in pink and white varieties, is elevated to
serve as a centerpiece for a dinner party.*

*'Paper-whites' are one of
the most reliable bulbs to force, blooming as early
as Christmas.*

$\mathcal{T}$o plant bulbs in an
open-work basket such as this, line it first with
sphagnum moss, then a sheet of plastic before
adding soilless potting mix and the bulbs.

own food supply makes fertilizer unnecessary, though tulips like a bit of bonemeal or a complete fertilizer. After your bulbs have bloomed, cut off the stems but let the leaves remain. Place the pots outdoors in a cool sunny spot and gradually stop watering. When the leaves have died, the bulbs will become dormant, and you can store them in a dry well-ventilated room at 60° to 70°F. In the fall, the bulbs can be transplanted into the garden, though they may need to restore their strength and may not bloom for a year or two. Bulbs forced in water are depleted and should be discarded.

PRE-COOLED BULBS

Pre-cooled bulbs, the fastest to bloom, are hardy bulbs that have already spent their cooling period {held at 40° to 50°F} before they are sold. This period usually occurs at the suppliers where they develop their roots. Pre-cooled bulbs are a particularly good choice for people who live in southern climates and can't readily provide the cooling period hardy bulbs need. Any hardy bulb can be pre-cooled, but seasonal availability varies, so be sure to check with your nursery or mail-order catalog as early as possible.

After purchasing the bulbs, keep them in a cool place {about 40° to 50°F} until the planting date. Count the pre-cooling period, and any time spent in a home refrigerator prior to potting, as part of the total cooling period.

FORCING TENDER BULBS

Certain tender bulbs do not require cooling and will grow and bloom naturally in the protection of a warm room. Set them in wet stones or soil and their roots appear almost instantly. 'Paper-white' narcissus, 'Soleil d'Or' narcissus, Chinese sacred lily, and amaryllis are a few of the bulbs that don't need cooling.

These plants are commonly grown in a soilless potting mix or on pebbles: fill a container that will not drain with soil, pebbles, gravel, or coarse sand so that it reaches to just an inch below the top; add water so that it is almost even with the planting medium, and place the bulb on top. Then, add more potting mix or pebbles so the bottom two-thirds of the bulbs are covered. Place the container in a cool {60°F} dark place until shoots develop~about two weeks. When shoots appear, move the plants into sunlight and water them regularly.

*Garnet-colored tulips are
late-winter bloomers when forced indoors. These
have been slipped into a brass kettle.*

Double-headed Tête-à-Tête' daffodils are massed together in this modern twig basket.

*Grape-hyacinths are
woodland flowers, and the twig basket echoes that
setting. The basket was woven of Scotch broom
and unpeeled willow.*

CHAPTER II

SYMBOLIC OF SPRING and renewal of the earth after a long winter, hardy bulbs hold a special place of
honor in the home. These harbingers of
warmer days carry sentimental associations and can adorn the home in a full
spectrum of color~from the most fiery
scarlet tulip to the palest yellow daffodil.

*For reasons only Nature
understands, bulbs started at the same time and
nurtured under identical conditions sometimes
grow at different rates.*

*A dozen and a half
'Unsurpassable' daffodils at their peak have been
planted in a rustic bark-covered container. The
blue and white painting behind them was
especially created by artist Michael Lane to play
up the lush yellow of the flowers.*

Forced hardy bulbs blooming indoors in midwinter, when the weather is gray and stormy, are especially delightful because they provide a delicious sense of "cheating the seasons." ℂ The characteristic that unites the bulbs in this chapter is their ability to grow outdoors in areas where freezing or near-freezing temperatures are common. Indeed, hardy bulbs require this cold spell to break their dormancy ∼ sometimes referred to as their rest period ∼ so that their growth can commence. Without it they will not bloom and gardeners who live in frost-free areas ∼ hardiness Zones 9 and 10, which include parts of the South, the Southwest, and the Pacific Coast ∼ can only enjoy these bulbs outdoors by cooling them in a refrigerator before planting. All they need do is place the bulbs in a refrigerator in their shipping bags or loose in the crisper at temperatures around 40°F for six to seven weeks for snowdrops and some smaller bulbs, twelve weeks or more for hyacinths, tulips and most other larger bulbs. Having a spare refrigerator on hand for this purpose is

A hyacinth is voluptuous~in color, form, and fragrance. These blooms will last several weeks under the right conditions.

recommended, since the bulbs may take up a lot of space and because they cannot be stored with certain fruits that emit ethylene gas, such as apples and pears.

As described in Chapter One, you can put your bulbs through a simulated winter by a cold treatment to bring them into bloom ahead of schedule. Forcing hardy bulbs in succession will provide you with cheerful bursts of bloom indoors from January to April. An additional benefit is that after being forced in soil ~ not in water ~ most of these spectacular plants can be transferred to the garden to flower in succeeding years. After the blooming, gradually reduce the amount of water you give them, but make sure the leaves remain, as they supply the sustenance for the bulb's future growth. Once the leaves have withered and turned brown, at the recommended time, plant them in the garden, and expect them to bloom in about two years.

CHIONODOXA, GLORY-OF-THE-SNOW

Chionodoxa, or glory-of-the-snow, is a true bulb that hails from the cold mountain meadows of Asia Minor and the mountains of Crete. This charming plant peeks through the soil just as the snow recedes. In fact, it was first discovered growing in melting snow in Asia Minor by Swiss botanist Pierre-Edmond Boissier a little more than one hundred years ago. When its starry flowers appear, they are vibrant blue or pink with white centers, pure white, or sky blue with about ten blossoms to six-inch stems. In the garden, the blooming season for these short-stemmed flowers lasts for three to four weeks in early spring, and they are most effective when planted in groups.

These delicately beautiful plants can be forced into midwinter bloom indoors, too. As soon as the bulbs become available, in late summer or early fall, pot twelve to fifteen of them in an eight-inch pot, bulb pan, or any other low, decorative container, with a soilless potting mix. Chionodoxa are hardy bulbs and must be allowed to root in a cool, dark place for at least fourteen weeks. Then bring the plants into indirect light, gradually exposing them to brighter sunlight once the buds appear. When the plant is in bloom, generally in late January, indirect light and cool temperatures will help prolong the flowering. If you want to enjoy the plant in a warm room, put it in a cooler room at night to keep the blooms as long as possible.

COLCHICUM, AUTUMN CROCUS

Colchicum, or autumn crocus, looks just like a crocus but is a member of the lily family, with six stamens instead of three. Instead of having grassy leaves like the true crocus, the colchicum has broad floppy leaves that appear after the plant has flowered. The English call colchicum "naked lady" because of its fleshy color and its leafless state when it flowers; the leaves don't appear until late winter.

Colchicum is a poisonous corm that blooms in the sunny garden in the fall. Despite the fact that it is a hardy bulb, it does not need a cooling period prior to forcing. These six-inch-tall plants can be forced~even without the benefit of water or soil~simply by bringing them into a warm room. Set on a saucer on a window sill, or in pebbles for a more "finished" look, autumn crocus produces delicate cup-shaped single or double blossoms of pink, lilac, pale mauve, or pure white in about two weeks. Be careful that they do not receive too much sunlight, which may burn the bulbs.

CONVALLARIA MAJALIS, LILY OF THE VALLEY

In the language of flowers, lilies of the valley signify the return of happiness. Native to Europe, these plants now grow wild in many parts of the world, favoring cool woods and shady places.

In the sixteenth century, the "wood lillie," as it was known, was prized for its medicinal properties. The flowers were distilled to make lily of the valley water, a common cure-all for gout, arthritis, sprains, and colic, and a featured ingredient in love potions. The plant is poisonous, and should be sited with care if there are children around. Planted in fall, lily of the valley enjoys having some shade and will bloom in late spring. The Dutch traditionally plant the garden of a newlywed couple with lily of the valley pips from the bride's bouquet, so the anniversary can be celebrated with this remembrance in sight.

Lily of the valley is a rhizome that sprouts in warmth, so its "pips" must be kept in cold storage before planting. Most lily of the valley pips sold for forcing are already pre-cooled when you buy them, and will bloom about three weeks after being planted. They bring a delightful fragrance to any room.

*L*ilies of the valley are
great unifiers, here transplanted to bring
harmony to an assortment of tea cups and
children's mugs.

The charming bell-shaped flowers with frilly edges are usually white, pink, or white tinged with pink. Lily of the valley is a small plant, growing to a height of nine inches at most, so group many of them together in a single pot for the finest showing. Plant them one inch deep in a shallow container filled with pebbles, equal parts loamy soil, peat, and sand, or soilless potting mix. A four- to six-inch deep pot is perfect for this fragrant plant. Place the growing tip so it just protrudes and keep at 60° to 65°F, or at least under 70°F, and in bright light.

CROCUS

The crocus is a cheerful addition to any garden; they are sprightly little plants, three to five inches tall. Known for their chalice-like forms, they appear in clear brilliant colors including lavender, purple, white, yellow, and orange, sometimes with a white or dark stripe down on the petals. They are members of the iris family and native to Mediterranean regions. Saffron, the spice and dye, comes from the dried stamen of the fall-blooming *Crocus sativus*.

Traditionally thought of as a harbinger of spring, some varieties do bloom in the garden in fall or winter.

Crocuses prefer sun, and are happy in a rock garden, planted amid shrubbery, in drifts on a hillside, or dotting a lawn.

The crocus is actually a corm, but for forcing purposes it can be treated similarly to a hyacinth bulb. Like the forced hyacinth, it can be planted in soil or in water in a clear glass crocus jar for a striking effect. Potted, pre-cooled, rooted crocuses will bloom in less than a month, or you may choose to cool them yourself. When potting, be sure to pack them closely together in soilless potting mix or sand, with the tops of the bulbs even with the rim of the pot. About fifteen crocuses will fit into a six- to eight-inch pot. Cool them for the recommended period, and once the roots have formed and the shoots are about two inches tall, put them in bright sunshine in a cool, 55°F room, to encourage blooms. You may feed crocuses lightly after their shoots are well developed.

Crocuses are ideal bulbs to grow indoors because warmth, not sun, causes them to open. In a warm room, even long after night has fallen, the flowers will still be open to enjoy. Almost all cultivars can be forced, but the lavender 'Remembrance,' 'Flower Record' and 'Victor Hugo,' white 'Joan of Arc' and 'Peter Pan,' and 'Large Yellow' are especially suitable.

HYACINTHUS, HYACINTH

Think hyacinth and fragrance comes to mind. This squat, foot-tall plant bears spires of thick flowers that give off a sweet, pervasive perfume. We have the Dutch to thank for this ~ they have been perfecting hyacinths for centuries. Folklore has it that one Dutchman was so enamored of his rare hyacinth that he hung it in a bird cage suspended from the ceiling in order to protect it from possible consumption by a rat or mouse. In the eighteenth century, Dutch hyacinths were so popular that they fetched a small fortune in England.

Hyacinths supposedly sprang from the blood of Hyacinthus when he was accidentally slain by Apollo, but botanists have found that the flower the Greeks commemorated in this myth more aptly described the lily, and not today's hyacinth.

According to garden writer Alice B. Coats, as early as 1682 it was observed by Nehemiah Grew that the flower buds of hyacinths and tulips were formed in the bulb during the previous season, and that it might be possible to make them bloom in winter "by keeping the plants warm, and thereby enticing the young lurking flowers to come abroad," {*The Anatomy of Plants*}. By 1730, Philip Miller at Chelsea Physic Garden in London, one of the world's oldest botanical gardens, was conducting experiments with the genus, and found that hyacinths grown in "common Thames water" performed better than tulips or narcissi.

Such pleasures can still be enjoyed by the indoor gardener. Large bulbs are easiest to force ~ they hold the most food. The larger the bulb, the larger the flower spike will be. Exhibition-size bulbs {at least 17cm} are popular choices for forcing or container planting, but smaller bulbs will also work. Dutch hyacinths are particularly well-suited to forcing and can be grown in well-drained soil, two or three bulbs to a five- to six-inch pot, with their tips near the surface or just protruding. They can also be grown on moist pebbles or marbles and water with the water just barely touching the base of the bulbs.

Like most hardy bulbs, hyacinths need a cooling period to form roots. Store the bulbs in a cool, dark place. The temperature should be less than 60°F; about 40° to 50°F is ideal. The exact length of the cooling period depends on the variety, but will be between ten and twelve weeks. After this period, pale flower buds appear on the spike. At this point, expose the bulbs to filtered light for a

'*Delft Blue*' *hyacinths*
in all their glory take pride of place in a sunny
Connecticut living room. The bovine weathervane
is of copper, from the turn of the century.

week or two. When the buds have turned green, expose them to full sun for at least four hours daily. For the remainder of the day, expose them to indirect, filtered sunlight. Try to guard against giving your hyacinths too much light too soon, or the plants will produce premature flowers on very short stems. When hyacinths are flowering, keep temperatures at 65°F or lower. In some regions, direct light may be too warm.

Another appealing way of forcing a hyacinth is in water alone, in a specially designed hyacinth glass that suspends the bulb just at the water line. This hydroponic forcing is possible because the hyacinth is one of the bulbs {along with crocus and narcissus} that stores so much food for the following year that it doesn't have to depend on soil nutrients, as do, for example, nearly all tulips. However, hydroponic forcing weakens the bulb, and it is discarded after flowering.

A clear, hourglass-shaped hyacinth container affords an "upstairs/downstairs" look at a bulb-in-progress, so you can monitor the growth of roots, leaves, and flowers. Keep the jar in a cool dark place {about 40° to 50° F} ~ such as a basement or cupboard ~ until full root development takes place and four-inch-tall buds appear ~ about twelve weeks, but possibly sooner. Adding a piece of activated charcoal to the water will inhibit algae growth and keep the water clear. Follow the steps for introducing the bulb to the warmth of the home and keep the water just touching the base of the bulb. A hyacinth bulb and hyacinth glass make a wonderful gift, especially for a child. But handling the bulb may irritate the skin, so take care to protect your hands and eyes.

Most hyacinths are suitable for forcing, including the smaller multiflora varieties; good cultivars include: blue 'Ostara' and 'Delft Blue,' white 'Innocence,' 'Pink Pearl,' and red 'Jan Bos' and 'Amsterdam'.

I R I S ,   M I N I A T U R E   I R I S

The beloved iris gets its name from the mythological Greek goddess of the rainbow, and the comparison is apt. These spring-flowering bulbs come in all colors of the rainbow, with sky blue to deep violet being the most popular and familiar range of hues. Only red is not represented in the iris spectrum.

These flowers are known as half-hardy bulbs, which means that they do not respond well to freezing but should be grown at a cool temperature. They bear appealingly shaped flowers which are known for their trio of upright petals {the "standards"} matched with three dropping petals {the "falls"}. Miniature iris, also called dwarf iris, flower outdoors in early spring. The diminutive *Iris reticulata* ~ which grows only three- to eight inches high ~ is one of the most popular of the miniature species. It is one of the first irises to bloom outdoors in early spring, and has been known to bloom on a southern exposure as early as late February. These small iris respond well to forcing, especially *Iris reticulata*, *Iris danfordiae*, and related species, which are preferred over Dutch iris.

Miniature iris require a short forcing period, sometimes as little as six to seven weeks. Force them as you would any hardy bulb, potting them early in the fall as soon as they become available, if possible. A dozen bulbs may be planted in a standard-size clay pot. Be sure to give your miniature iris plants a well-drained soil but don't let the soil dry out.

MUSCARI, GRAPE-HYACINTH

There is a woodland feel about the tiny grape-hyacinth, with its urn-shaped clusters of flowers nodding gently atop slender stems. The grape-hyacinth is a member of the lily family, and is a true bulb. It hails from Europe, the Mediterranean, and adjacent regions. Some grape-hyacinths have a sweet scent; others have no fragrance.

Describing *Muscari botryoides* in his work *Prosperina*, late-nineteenth century English author John Ruskin wrote that its scent was "as if a cluster of grapes and a hive of honey had been distilled and pressed together in one small boss of celled and beaded blue." Grape-hyacinths are most often blue, ranging from pale azure to a deep violet, but can also be white, and grow six- to nine-inches high. When massed together, they make a beautiful border or blanket of blue for the spring garden, and can also

Miniature Iris reticulata are perfect for tabletop arrangements. Here they lend their intense colors to a corner used for everything from game playing to letter writing.

be tucked beneath trees or grown in pots. Cobalt-blue *Muscari armeniacum* is the most commonly grown variety, both indoors and out, and is the best variety for forcing early.

Grape-hyacinths are hardy bulbs; depending on the variety, they need a cooling period of at least eight weeks. Pot them in the fall, with the tips just below the surface of the soil, packing up to a dozen bulbs in a six-inch pot of well-drained soil. Grape-hyacinths are small bulbs, and look quite charming when crowded this way. As with other hardy bulbs, set the potted bulbs in the dark to develop their roots, keeping them moist during this cooling period; expose them to full sun for about four hours daily when stems and foliage show. When the buds show color and begin to open, indirect light and cool temperatures will help prolong the flowers.

N A R C I S S U S ,
D A F F O D I L

Daffodil is the common name for the majority of trumpet-shaped flowers of the well-loved genus of true bulbs known botanically as *Narcissus*. Within this genus there are many classifications based on plant structure, and other common names such as jonquil are used for specific groups. For our purposes, however, daffodil is the all-encompassing term for these spring bloomers. {For a discussion of tender plants known commonly as "narcissus" including the 'Paper-white' variety, see Chapter Three.}

Despite their pert appearance, daffodils are hardy, reliable performers in the garden, dependably blooming year after year and relatively immune to diseases and pests. Daffodils are known for their cheerful trumpet- or cup-shaped flowers which come in almost every shade of yellow, from deep egg-yolk to palest lemon, as well as pure white.

Most narcissi originated in Spain, Portugal, and North Africa. The brief spring rains and long dry summers of this Mediterranean area account for the narcissus' preference for well-drained, sandy soil. Narcissi produce their best blooms after plenty of rain, but, like most bulbs, they will rot if left sitting in waterlogged soil. To protect against basal rot, gardeners in warm climates sometimes dip narcissus bulbs in a solution containing a substance known as "formalin"~which contains formaldehyde~before they are planted. When narcissus does succumb to a virus {signaled by yellow or white stripes on the foliage}, dig up the bulb and discard it.

*The muted palette of this
living room fireplace benefits from the splash of
color some grape-hyacinths add.*

*'Geranium' daffodils rest
cozily in an egg-gathering basket set upon an
antique wood pedestal. The massive Dutch
cupboard dates from 1780.*

*D*affodils planted in
hand-thrown, nineteenth-century pots are nestled
among the antiques displayed on the shelves of a
converted buttery.

To force hardy narcissi, pot them closely using a soilless potting mix, set them in a dark unheated spot 40° to 50° F to root for fourteen weeks, and then bring them out into the light. Ideally, daffodils should be exposed to the very bright light of a greenhouse at temperatures of 40° to 50°F. However, an enclosed sunroom or porch or direct light from a skylight make acceptable substitutes; northern light or diffused light is not recommended, as a lack of sun results in leggy growth and no blossoms.

After the flowers have bloomed, the bulbs can be transplanted into the garden, but it may take two or three years for them to reach full blooming potential. Remove spent blooms and continue watering and feeding with a water-soluble fertilizer until foliage withers. Remove the bulbs from the pot and plant in the garden in the fall.

The "noses" on your narcissus bulb indicate how many blooms you can expect. A triple-nosed bulb will produce three flowers; a double-nosed bulb, two flowers; the single-nose bulb, one flower. Keep in mind that miniature daffodils have smaller bulbs than do standard-size daffodils and when potting them, you can crowd as many as twelve bulbs in a six- to eight-inch bulb pan or pot, whereas if you decide to grow larger types, you may be limited to three to five bulbs per container.

Miniature daffodils are widely considered to be the best hardy types for forcing at home. 'Tête-à-Tête,' 'February Gold,' 'Jumblie,' 'WeeBee,' and 'Minnow' are among the varieties to look for. More adventurous gardeners might want to experiment with the large orange-yellow 'Flower Record,' the large all-yellow 'Dutch Master,' the double white 'Bridal Crown,' or the cream-white, large-cupped 'Ice Follies.'

The transition of the seasons is marked by parallel natural gestures: on an oversize ottoman, a silver bowl of pomanders represents winter and, opposite, a sphagnum basket of 'Ice Follies' narcissus augurs spring.

*Tiny Scilla siberica is so
diminutive that it must be placed prominently in
a room.*

SCILLA, BLUEBELLS

Delicate bluebells, more correctly called scilla or squills, are true bulbs native to Western Europe and northern Africa. Most of the bluebells found in gardens today are hybrids of English or Spanish species. English bluebells are fragrant, usually blue, and hang from slightly arching stems. Spanish bluebells are not fragrant; come in shades of purple, pink, or white; and have taller, upright stems up to eighteen inches long.

Bluebells will tolerate almost any exposure outdoors, from filtered shade to full sun. Gardeners usually grow them in naturalistic plantings, owing to their rustic appearance, grouped together for impact in rock gardens or scattered across a lawn or the edges of woodland.

Scilla tubergeniana and *Scilla siberia* are the most popular scilla to force, producing tiny blue or white flowers on delicate four- or five-inch stems. They require a forcing period of six to seven weeks before being brought into indirect light. Plant bluebells closely; you can fit about a dozen of these small bulbs in a six- to eight-inch pot, bulb pan, or any other attractive container in a standard potting medium. Storing the pots in the coolest room in the house {with temperatures of 50° F or less at night} will make the blooms last longer. Keep the soil moist during active growth and do not fertilize.

TULIPA, TULIPS

The tulip is a member of the lily family, native to central Asia and Europe. From its early days as a plant for the rich and royal, the tulip has developed into one of the most popular and well-known of all the spring bulbs.

In 1554, a tulip mania began in Europe when an Austrian ambassador imported tulips from Constantinople. People gambled and speculated over tulip bulbs, and fortunes were won and lost. During the years 1634 through 1637, it was not uncommon for bulbs to double in price from one day to the next.

Outdoors, tulips grow best in full sun or very light shade; plant them four to eight inches deep, depending on the size of bulbs, and space them three to six inches apart. There are hundreds of different types of tulips, in almost every color and some bi-colors too, and new hybrids appear annually. But species tulips ~ the ones that grow naturally in Asia Minor and Europe ~ are often more robust and dependable than the hybrids. Both species tulips and hybrid tulips are

*Cool white 'Snow
Star' tulips, an Early American box, a bowl of
potpourri, and a young girl's photograph complete
a library still-life.*

*A handmade child's
chair from Mexico is just the right size for a box
of tulips. Several hours of sunlight each day will
encourage rapid growth of the grass as well as the
bulbs.*

*The colors and textures of
flowers can be played against those of a room,
producing surprisingly harmonious arrangements.*

well adapted to forcing. Cultivars that tend to force well include 'Attila' {lavender}, 'Apricot Beauty' {apricot}, 'Bellona' {deep yellow}, 'Christmas Marvel' {cherry pink}, 'Pax' {white}, and 'Lucky Strike' {red and white bi-color}.

Ask your nursery or garden center for help in finding the most suitable tulips for forcing. Choose "top size" bulbs~about 12cm~with plenty of papery brown skin to protect the bulb from drying out. Avoid bulbs with green shoots; this growth should not occur until the roots are firmly established. Early-blooming varieties~like single and double early tulips~will be among the first to brighten the winter home indoors, but mid- and late-season bloomers can also be forced to give you a nonstop display of flowers.

Specially prepared, pre-cooled early tulips are available, requiring only two weeks of cool darkness before being brought into the light. But most tulips require a long, sustained cooling period~at least fifteen weeks~in order to establish an expansive root system. Without good roots, tulips cannot produce spectacular blossoms, so let the roots grow as long as possible. {Rodents love to munch on tulip bulbs. Keep the bulbs protected if you're cooling them in containers outdoors.}

When shoots appear, move the pots to a cool spot {55° to 65° F} away from direct light. After buds are well formed, put the pots in direct light by a window. At this point, tulips can be fed with a fertilizer containing calcium. As the flowers begin to show color, take them out of direct light to lengthen the life of the blooms.

Planting bulbs shoulder-to-shoulder helps ensure a beautiful showing and the roots will tend to support each other. In a six-inch container, for instance, pack a half-dozen tulips with their tips even with the rim of the pot. Bulbs circling the edge of the pot should be positioned so their flat side faces out. This way, each plant's first large leaf will drape over the edge of the pot.

'Jingle Bells' is one tulip cultivar that deserves special mention. It has been developed to grow very fast in water alone. Usually, this cultivar does not need cold treatment as they are sold pre-cooled. Within a week, they will develop roots and will bloom after three weeks. Because of their short life, they are usually sold through the mail, shipping in early December for Christmas blooming.

M irroring the pale
shades of a stained glass window by Allan Shope,
left, a pot of 'New Design' tulips have been in
bloom for about a week.

Bright yellow tulips on an antique Korean
chest, right, make a bold contrast against their
rough cast cement planter.

*In their eighteenth-
century cottage, Robert Kinnaman and Brian
Ramaekers display a basket of tulips, left,
on an Early American blanket chest.*

*A graceful terra-cotta pot, right, cradles compact
orange 'Flair' tulips. Behind the bulbs is a bas
relief entitled 'Allegory of Art.'*

THE BULBS INCLUDED in this chapter ～ from the stunning, brilliantly colored amaryllis to the diminutive rhodohypoxis ～ are generally classified as "tender" bulbs. This means that they can't withstand being grown outdoors year-round in cool climates ～ a minimum 10° to 20°F. Some are technically considered

Twin agapanthus in identical clay pots share a corner of a music room with a Louisiana lollin' chair.

*Exhibiting colors most
artists would be happy to duplicate, velvety-red
gloxinia flowers complement the deep green leaves
of the plant.*

"half-hardy"~or "half-tender," if you prefer~which means that they are of subtropical origin and can only be grown outdoors in certain hardiness zones and are intolerant of frost~but do need to be exposed to cool conditions to flower successfully. Examples are agapanthus and freesia, which are South African bulbs, sometimes also called Cape bulbs. Other bulbs are native to tropical places and are extremely tender. These plants are particularly easy to make bloom indoors as house-plants. Examples include amaryllis, gloxinia, and *Narcissus tazetta* varieties such as 'Paper-white' and 'Soleil d'Or.' ℂ Generally speaking, the plants included in this chapter thrive in 55° to 65°F temperatures and enjoy sunny locations in the home or the greenhouse. Grow them in an unheated, glassed-in sun-porch or on a windowsill in a moderately cool room. They respond well to frequent watering during their growth period as well as weekly feedings with a houseplant fertilizer, cut back to half strength. They also enjoy humidity, so consider placing the potted bulbs on a tray filled with pebbles and water; when they are growing, rotate them daily so that the plants do not lean toward the sun. Once in bloom, move them into actively lived-in areas of the house to brighten and cheer rooms.

Because they are native to varied environments~including South and Central America, South America, and tropical regions of the world~there are many ways to grow these plants in containers. Half-hardy bulbs like agapanthus and alstroemeria make good "indoor-outdoor" plants: they can be brought into the yard or onto the terrace in summer and spend the winter indoors or in a sheltered porch. In warm climates~Zones 9 and 10~such as most of Southern California, all the bulbs that follow can be grown outdoors in pots year-round {if they are planted in the garden, however, they can weather the winter in Zones 7 to 10}. Very tender bulbs, such as clivia, are quite sensitive to cold and must be kept indoors year-round as houseplants, unless you live in Zone 10 {southern Florida}.

There are also several methods of caring for and bringing the bulbs into bloom. 'Paper-white' narcissus is forced to bloom by a method similar to standard forcing of hardy bulbs. The principal difference is that it does not undergo an extensive cooling period and blooms in sunlight. Others, such as clivia, only need to be potted and placed in indirect sunlight. Ranunculus and anemone prefer to be potted and placed in a cool, dark place for a short time before being moved into sunlight. Read the descriptions in this chapter carefully before growing any of these plants. The listings that follow include only a selection of the better-known or easier bulbs to bring to bloom indoors in containers. Other tender plants that you may wish to grow indoors in a similar fashion include achimenes, sparaxis, the calla lily, eucharis, haemanthus, and nerine.

A G A P A N T H U S , L I L Y O F T H E N I L E

Lily of the Nile, the evocative common name for members of the marvelous *Agapanthus* genus, conjures up visions of serene lagoons, exotic birds, and lush jungles. Actually, agapanthus is a native of South Africa, but in every way it measures up to the romantic associations its name suggests. This prized bulb sends up stunning clusters of one- to four-inch blue or white flowers on plants that average two feet tall, making it a dramatic plant for container culture.

One of the tallest
flowering plants, agapanthus has a grace and
delicacy that combine beautifully with its height.

There are two basic categories of agapanthus~the deciduous type, which loses its leaves but can be grown outdoors in a wide range of hardiness zones, and the evergreen varieties, which are more tender yet are popular as houseplants and tend to be more readily available from garden suppliers. For this reason, we will address only the evergreen type here. The most popular evergreen species are *Agapanthus praecox orientalis*, which may grow as high as five feet and has blue or white flowers, and *Agapanthus africanus* {also known as *umbellatus*}, which has deep blue flowers and tends to grow a foot and a half to two feet tall. These agapanthuses can be grown outdoors in pots year-round in Zones 9 and 10, but need to be brought indoors at the first sign of frost in other zones. Alternatively, they can be grown year-round indoors as houseplants.

To grow agapanthus, plant the bulbs anytime from February to April for late spring or summer bloom. Select a clay pot large enough to accommodate the roots but not much larger. The plant blooms more abundantly when its roots are slightly crowded. A good rule of thumb is to grow one plant in an eight-inch pot or three in a twelve-inch pot. Place the bulbs so that the crowns are just above the planting medium. A po-

rous medium usually works best~one that contains about one part potting soil, one part peat moss, and one part sharp sand with limestone added.

Give the plants a thorough watering, then let them root in a cool place with temperatures in the 55° F range in a sun-filtered location. During this period, water them regularly but not excessively. When the foliage and flower stalk emerge, transfer the plants to a bright yet still-cool location and increase watering; feed them every two weeks or so with a standard houseplant fertilizer. After the plants bloom, continue watering minimally to preserve the evergreen foliage but do not fertilize them. When the leaves wither, put the plants in a cool {45° F} location through winter, and in the spring, water and fertilize again.

ALSTROEMERIA, PERUVIAN LILY

The lovely Peruvian lily~a South American native, as its name implies~is often mistaken for a true lily. But in fact the Peruvian lily is unto itself in the genus *Alstroemeria*. There are about half a dozen species of Peruvian lilies available and they are steadily gaining popularity.

Colors include delicate yellows and oranges and more flamboyant pinks and fiery reds. The flowers bloom on one- to four-foot-tall stalks with as many as fifty to a cluster.

Peruvian lilies are half-hardy plants, which means that they enjoy a cool rooting period before flowering. They can be grown outdoors in pots year-round in Zones 7 through 10~protected from temperatures below 40° F~and need to be brought indoors at the first sign of frost in other zones.

To grow your own Peruvian lilies, plant the tuberous roots in fall in eight- to twelve-inch clay pots. A recommended planting mixture is one part potting soil, one part sharp sand, and one part peat moss. Water the bulbs thoroughly and place them in a cool location ~around 55" F~to root in half light.

When they show signs of growth, begin watering them frequently and fertilize them weekly or every other week. Transfer them to a sunny location and continue to feed and water them as instructed until they bloom. During their blooming period in spring, feed them monthly. After they have bloomed, gradually cut back watering and fertilizing until the leaves wither. Then, place them in a dry cool location, with temperatures around 40° F. Begin watering and fertilizing again in the following spring.

A N E M O N E ,
W I N D F L O W E R

Rich jewel-colored petals and slender furry stems give anemones their ethereal quality. Some historians believe that the biblical "lilies of the field" were actually anemones.

Some anemones are poppy-like; others look more like daisies. Anemones are members of the buttercup family. Like the crocus, the anemone opens in sunlight and closes at night and in cloudy weather. This means that anemones will stay open long after dark in a warm room with the lights on~a colorful sight of white, pink, red, blue, or purple petals. Flame or peacock anemones {*Anemone coronaria*}, sometimes called florists' anemones, are the most dramatic, known for their foot-tall stems and two-inch flowers. These can be grown by a method similar to forcing hardy bulbs.

Begin forcing anemones indoors in September. Soak the tubers in tepid water twenty-four hours before planting them, a half dozen to a six-inch pot of moistened, well-drained potting soil. Claw-shaped tubers should be planted claws down. If it is hard to tell which end goes up or down, plant them sideways. Set the pots outdoors in cool shade until the first light frost, then place them in a cool, 40° to 50° F window with indirect light. Water them lightly until their growth is several inches tall. Keep the soil evenly moist and fertilize them regularly as their leaves and flowers develop. To produce the best flowers, cool temperatures are critical. {Warmer temperatures speed growth, but smaller flowers and shorter stems will result.}

After blooming, when the leaves die down, reduce watering. Store the bulbs in a cool, dark spot until September. In the fall, repot the bulbs and begin feeding and watering again.

CLIVIA, KAFFIR LILY

Clivia ∼ the Kaffir lily ∼ is a South African native that sends forth umbels of magnificent flowers in late winter and early spring, when it has been grown as a houseplant. It is a highly popular, undemanding plant for indoor gardening. Strap-like evergreen leaves surround bright, showy orange, scarlet, salmon, yellow, or gold blossoms on a one-and-a half- to two-foot stem.

The fleshy roots of the Kaffir lily are best planted in spring. Set the roots just below the surface of a rich potting mixture of equal parts soil and peat. Fan out the roots over the mixture and just barely cover them with soil. Water the plant thoroughly and set it in a room with indirect sunlight and high humidity. It enjoys day temperatures of 60° to 72° F and a night temperature of about 50° F when it is blooming ∼ although the plant is tolerant of a range of conditions.

In spring and summer, feed clivia monthly with houseplant fertilizer and water it weekly. After the plant blooms, water it less frequently. "Dry off" the plant by decreasing watering beginning in the fall, when it is setting buds, and on into winter. At this time, eliminate the feedings. Keep clivia in temperatures of 45° to 50° F . When a new leaf forms in the center, bring the plant into a warmer room and increase watering.

Root-bound plants are the best bloomers, so resist the impulse to transplant them more than once every three to four years.

CYCLAMEN, FLORISTS' CYCLAMEN

A beautiful cyclamen is a glorious and much appreciated Christmas or Valentine's Day gift. It is one of the prettiest

Cyclamen blossoms
appear atop slender, auburn stems. Even when not
in bloom, this large genus of plants is interesting
for its intricately variegated leaves.

houseplants plants and stays in bloom continuously from October through April, if you give the plant proper care.

The florists' or Persian cyclamen {*Cyclamen persicum* hybrids} is usually grown as a houseplant, though it can be grown outdoors at temperatures above 20° F. The plant is noted for its heart- or kidney-shaped silver-marked leaves. It grows four to eight inches tall and bears white, purple, red, pink, rose, or salmon flowers; some of which can be bicolored.

Because the seeds take fifteen to eighteen months to bloom, most people purchase the plant from a florist when it is in flower, although newly developed dwarf hybrids take only six to eight months. However, you can also grow the plant from tubers. These must be carefully handled before planting, because the new growth that appears as small bumps on the tuber can easily be broken off, and it then takes at least a year for the bulb to send out new growth again. Plant one tuber per four-inch pot in a mixture of two parts peat moss, one part sharp sand, and one part potting soil. Water well and then set the plants in a room with cool temperatures ~ around 55° to 65° F during the day, and as low as 40° F at night ~ that is indirectly lit by sun. Cyclamen favors an eastern exposure. Water them regularly and feed them monthly with houseplant fertilizer.

After the blooming ends in the spring, decrease watering and allow the plant to dry off. Store them in the pots in a dark place. Keep the soil just barely moist until sprouting begins in the fall.

DAHLIA

The clear, vibrant colors of dahlia flowers ~ including scarlet, hot pink, and brilliant yellow ~ suggest their Mexican origins. When cultivating these tubers, you must keep in mind that they are only hardy to Zone 9 outdoors, and their roots must be protected from frost. Therefore, if you set your pots outside in summer, bring them in before the first frost.

There are about thirty species in this genus. The standard types can grow to seven feet high and are beautiful when massed in the garden border. Miniature

A freshly transplanted red dahlia is about to be moved from the porch to the house.

77

*Freesias the color of
goldenrod nestle in the eaves of an attic bedroom.*

dahlias, such as the patio and windowsill types, have charming, compact blossoms only twelve to twenty inches high and are no more than four inches in diameter~and often as little as in inch around. Because of their diminutive size, these are easy to cultivate in containers. 'Unwin's Dwarf' dahlias~in red, lavender, and yellow~lend themselves particularly well to pot culture: they grow only to eighteeen inches, and the flowers are two inches across. *Dahlia pinnata* hybrids come in dwarf varieties that grow a foot high in hues of yellow, red, pink, orange, and white; some are even bi-colored.

To cultivate miniature dahlias in pots, give them a well-drained potting soil. Place three tubers in an eight-inch pot, with tubers laid horizontally and just below the surface. Water thoroughly and place them in semi-darkness in a room with temperatures around 60° to 65° F to undergo their rooting period. Once top growth begins, bring them out into a location that gets at least four hours of direct sunlight a day. Water them regularly and apply a standard household fertilizer weekly. After the plants have bloomed, cut back on watering to dry off and let them rest for the winter in a cool, dark place with 50° F temperatures. Resume their watering and feeding in early spring.

FREESIA

This South African native is a tender corm that is quite easy to grow indoors for bloom in winter and spring. Flowers blossom on slender eighteen-inch stems, with bell-shaped blossoms in almost every known flower color, including white. The smaller white and yellow freesias are generally more fragrant than the newer hybrids, and despite freesia's reputation, some large-flowered freesias have almost no scent at all.

Plant six teardrop-shaped freesia corms per six-inch pot. Potting a batch of corms every few weeks from August to December will ensure flowers from December to March. Plant the corms pointed side up, just beneath the surface of a planting medium that's been dusted with ground limestone.

Water the plants thoroughly and place the pots in a dark place, with temperatures in the 40° to 50° F range. After four to six weeks, top growth should appear and freesia can be brought to a cool, sunny spot.

Freesias need plenty of sunshine~ideally about eight to ten hours daily~and at least ten to twelve weeks of growing time before they will bloom. A greenhouse or cool sunroom is an ideal place for growing freesia.

When the blooms stop coming and the foliage withers, gradually stop watering. Place the pots in a cool, dry place. Then, in the fall, repot them and begin watering and feeding to initiate new growth.

G L A D I O L U S

Gladiolus hails from south and central Africa, where the species plants grow wild. It is a stately flower, known for its tall spikes of blossoms and its sword-like leaves; in fact, the word "gladiolus" means small sword in Latin. These spectacular plants have a complex heritage, and there are more than two hundred and fifty species, as well as thousands of named forms. There are two types of gladioli: some bloom in summer{this includes the common garden gladiolus}and the others bloom in late winter and early spring. They come in almost every color imaginable, including green and smoky brown; only a true blue has yet to be developed. The plants grow one to six feet tall, with flowers up to six inches wide, depending on the variety. For the purposes of indoor gardening, however, you should select smaller gladioli.

The late-winter- and early-spring-blooming species, such as *Gladiolus* x *Colvillei and G. tristis* {evening-flowering gladiolus}, can be forced for winter bloom. They are both small varieties. The evening-flowering gladiolus, as its name implies, blooms at night. Three to four small, fragrant, creamy white or yellow flowers with purple markings bloom on one stalk. This species grows only to two feet and has slender, long leaves.

In September and October, put five corms in a six-inch pot using a well-drained, moistened potting mix and setting them two inches deep. Set them in a cool, dark place with temperatures around 40° to 50°F. Water them thoroughly. After six weeks, bring them into a cool {50°F}bright room, and keep the soil barely moist. More water is necessary as plants enter full growth and flowering. Feed them regularly. After the flowers fade and foliage yellows, stop watering and remove the corms from the pot. Store them in a cool, dark place until the following fall. Repot the corms during dormancy. Begin watering again when the plant emerges from dormancy in the following fall.

H I P P E A S T R U M , A M A R Y L L I S

Amaryllis are a familiar herald of Christmas time. This huge bulb is

*A cool white 'Ludwig's
Dazzler' amaryllis echoes the stillness of a white
bedroom. A heavy stoneware jug provides enough
support for the amaryllis.*

known for its bold trumpet blooms, which burst forth from atop a tall, strong stalk. The striking six- to ten-inch broad amaryllis blooms come in many colors ~red, pink, orange, salmon, or white.

To grow amaryllis, use a pot that is only slightly larger than the bulb. Leave about a one-inch space between the bulb and the edge of the flower pot. This ensures vigorous flower growth, while limiting the growth of leaves. Use well-drained potting soil~some experts recommend adding one part peat moss or perlite to the mixture. Plant the bulb so the top two-thirds of it protrudes from the soil and the roots are in the soil.

Place the potted bulb in a warm, well-lit place and water it well. Do not water it again until the growth begins and a bud emerges from the center of the plant. It's almost impossible to predict how long this will take since each amaryllis bulb seems to be on its own schedule. Sometimes bud growth will commence immediately; other times, a month or more may pass before this happens. Increase the amount of water as the plant grows and keep the soil damp. Every few days, rotate the pot to keep the stalk from leaning toward the light. This produces a more stately, upright effect. Generally speaking, the amaryllis should bloom in five to six weeks. When the plant

flowers, move it to a cool, shaded location, as this will lengthen the life of the blossoms about two weeks.

To make the amaryllis bloom again the following year, cut off the flowers after they have withered, leaving the stalk and foliage. Set the plant in a sunny window and treat it as you would any foliage houseplant. Water and fertilize it regularly. The pot can also be moved outdoors into filtered shade after the danger of frost is past.

Whether it is kept indoors or outdoors, amaryllis will go dormant in late summer. The leaves and stalks will turn yellow and die. At this point, remove the leaves from the top of the bulb and stop watering and fertilizing. If it was outdoors, bring the pot inside and store it in a cool place such as a basement.

Four or five weeks before you want your amaryllis to bloom~generally around Thanksgiving~add a top layer of fresh planting medium and resume watering. Repot every few years.

Sometimes it is necessary to place a stake in the pot, to help support the large top-heavy flower stalk. Although the amaryllis is commonly thought of as a Christmas flower, it can also be grown outdoors in warmer climates~Zones 9 and 10. Planted in the early spring, it usually blooms in May.

*An old mushroom
basket has been filled with 'Paper-whites' and
brought into a sunny living room. Before the
bulbs were planted, the basket was lined with
plastic to prevent seepage.*

*R anunculus, above, a
distant relative of the buttercup, is one of the most
endearing of tender summer bulbs.*

NARCISSUS TAZETTA

In addition to the hardy narcissi, there are several varieties of tender *Narcissus tazetta* that can be grown indoors for winter bloom. The most beloved of these flowers is the elegant, snow-colored 'Paper-white' narcissus. Yellow 'Soleil d'Or' and Chinese sacred lily, which is white with a golden yellow interior, are also popular narcissi for forcing. They can provide indoor blooms from November through March if planted successively, batch after batch, in the late fall, and will produce powerfully fragrant flowers atop eighteen-inch stems in four to six weeks.

Plant these narcissus varieties in a pan or bowl that does not have drainage holes and is filled with pebbles or perlite, or in a regular pot in well-drained potting soil. In soil, the nose of the bulb should be even with, or slightly above, the rim of the pot. In pebbles, sand, or perlite, water should just barely touch the bottoms of the bulbs; maintain the water level as necessary.

'Soleil d'Or' and Chinese sacred lily need to develop their roots in a dark, cool place~between 50° and 60° F~for ten days after potting. In about two weeks, when the bulbs and are about three inches high, bring them out into the light.

Once the sweet-scented blossoms of any of these narcissi appear, cool temperatures and indirect light will make the flowers last longer; the flowers will bloom for about two weeks. In climates where the ground does not freeze in winter, tender narcissi grown in soil fertilized regularly have been known to bloom again after forcing. For the average gardener, however, these bulbs cannot be replanted: consider them a midwinter treat and discard them when spent.

RANUNCULUS, PERSIAN BUTTERCUP

The ranunculus, commonly known as the Persian buttercup, grows around the world. Even the tropical species appear in mountains, displaying the plant's fondness for cool weather. Outdoors in the northeastern United States, the ranunculus blooms in May and June; plants in pots may bloom up to four weeks earlier.

This plant is a tuberous root that produces multi-petaled flowers of yellow, orange, pink, red, and white, on ten- to twelve-inch stalks, with graceful, fern-like foliage.

Before planting the tubers in containers, soak them in water for three or four hours; this encourages faster sprouting. They prefer potting soil with added sand for drainage~a mixture of equal parts loam, sand, and peat works well. Plant six tubers to a six-inch pot, claws down. Water them thoroughly once, then place the pots in a dark, cool location with temperatures in the 40° to 50°F range~a cool greenhouse or sunroom is an ideal location. Water them minimally during this period, which should be about four to six weeks. When signs of top growth appear, step up the watering and place the plants in a location that receives four hours of direct sunlight daily yet is relatively cool~in the 50° to 60°F range. Feed them with houseplant fertilizer at half strength until the blooms have faded. When the foliage begins to wither, gradually cut back on watering and allow the plants to go dormant. Transfer the pots to a cool, dry place and leave them there until fall, when you can repot the tubers and begin watering and fertilizing again.

R H O D O H Y P O X I S B A U R I I

For those who wish to collect out-of-the ordinary bulbs for indoor culture, rhodo-hypoxis is a wonderful choice. It has only recently been made available and therefore is a particularly novel plant to display in the home. Of course, gardeners have also found uses for it outdoors, growing it in rock gardens and between cracks in flagstone paths. Because it is a South African native, however, it doesn't tolerate temperatures below 10°F, so gardeners north of Zone 8 must take the plant indoors in cold weather.

Rhodohypoxis tends to grow no more than four inches high, and so this diminutive plant is a natural choice for planting in bonsai pots. Its lovely flowers form a six-pointed star and are available in white and soft pink and rose shades.

To grow this charming plant indoors, obtain bulbs for late winter or early spring potting. Plant them an inch apart, one half to one inch deep, in a well-drained potting mix. Give the plants a thorough watering, then place them in a cool room {temperatures around 55° to 65°F} with indirect light. When the plants show signs of growth, transfer them to a bright yet still-cool location and increase watering and feed them with a standard houseplant fertilizer. During the spring and summer growth and blooming periods, water rhodo-hypoxis generously and feed monthly. After the plants bloom and the leaves

A n unusual tiny tender
bulb, rhodohypoxis flowers have been massed
together in an unfinished-wood box that plays up
the plant's unassuming nature.

*A wood-gathering basket
has been selected for three red and white gloxinias.
The low-set windows of this eighteenth-century
house flood the plant with light.*

begin to wither, begin to reduce watering and feeding. Transfer them to a cool, dark spot {about 45°F} that does not freeze. Although you must decrease watering, do not let the plants dry out. Resume watering in late winter, when growth starts, and bring them into a cool room with bright, indirect light.

SINNINGIA, GLOXINIA

Gloxinias are hybridized versions of Brazilian wildflowers and have inherited the unpredictability of untamed species. These South American natives may bloom once or twice a year in any season~the species *Sinningia pusila* sometimes blooms all year long~but can generally be expected to go dormant in the fall and winter.

These showy houseplants grow a foot high and produce velvety bell- or slipper-shaped flowers about three to four inches long. Their intense colors are vivid red, purple, violet, pink, or white. There are also types with white edges, blotches, or other markings. The broad four- to six-inch hairy leaves are brittle and break off easily, so handle your gloxinia with care.

You can begin to grow gloxinias at any time from February to August. Plant the tubers concave side up, one tuber to a six-inch pot, in well-drained potting soil. African violet soil is ideal{the two plants are closely related},a mixture of one part peat moss and one part potting soil is fine. Each tuber should be covered with no more than an inch of the planting medium. Water them well, and keep the soil barely moist, making sure the foliage and flowers don't get wet; the plants are sensitive to excess moisture.

Gloxinias enjoy bright indirect sunlight, and can also be grown under fluorescent plant lights with fourteen to sixteen hours of exposure each day. They also appreciate warmth. Day temperatures of 70° to 75°F suit gloxinia just fine; night temperatures shouldn't fall below 65°F.

Fertilize them twice monthly during growth and bloom. When the leaves begin to wither, this is your signal that the plants' dormant period is beginning. Withhold their food and decrease water gradually, but never let the soil dry completely. The leaves will eventually drop off. Let the plant rest undisturbed in a cool basement or closet. New growth will emerge in two to four months. Then resume regular watering and feeding, usually in January.

YOU ARE ENSURED the greatest success with bulbs if you buy those designated as "suitable for forcing." In placing an order from a catalog, look for this distinction and also order the largest bulbs available, since these tend to produce the most beautiful flowers.

BULBS SOURCES

Amaryllis, Inc.
1452 Glenmore Avenue
P.O. Box 318
Baton Rouge, LA 70821
504-924-5560
A variety of amaryllis bulbs pre-cooled and suitable for forcing; a good selection of size and colors.

Bakker of Holland
Louisiana, MO 63353
314-754-4525
The major varieties of bulbs and a listing of hardy and tender miscellaneous bulbs.

Breck's
6523 N. Galena Road
Peoria, IL 61632
309-691-4616
One of the country's leading suppliers of bulbs; pre-cooled and varieties for forcing are available.

Bundles of Bulbs
112 Greenspring Valley Road
Owings Mills, MD 21117
301-363-1371
Scores of tulips, narcissi, lilies, and other bulbs for fall planting; catalog notes which bulbs are suitable for forcing.

W. Atlee Burpee Company
300 Park Avenue
Warminster, PA 18974
800-333-5808
The largest of all the mail-order gardening suppliers, with bulbs for forcing and pre-cooled bulbs.

Daffodil Mart
Route 3, Box 794
Gloucester, VA 23061
804-693-3966
Almost 400 varieties of daffodils listed by flower type, color, bloom season and height in their informative catalog. Some varieties can be forced indoors.

Peter de Jager Bulb Co.
188 Asbury Street
Box 2010
South Hamilton, MA 01982
508-468-4707
Varieties of hyacinths and tulips suitable for forcing.

Dutch Gardens, Inc.
P.O. Box 200
Adelphia, NJ 07710
201-391-4366
A strong list of selections which includes gloxinia and lily for indoor growing; amaryllis, daffodil, hyacinth, and narcissus for forcing and an indoor forcing collection kit with 42 bulbs including tulips, irises, and crocus.

French's, Bulb Importer
Route 100
Pittsfield, VT 05762
802-746-8148
A good selection of imported bulbs, including unusual varieties and pre-cooled.

Gladside Gardens
61 Main Street
Northfield, MA 01360
413-498-2657
Gladiolus, lily, and anemone for indoor growing.

John D. Lyon, Inc.
143 Alewife Brook Parkway
Cambridge, MA 02140
617-876-3705
Specialty in crocus plus many other varieties such as allium, anemone, freesia, and scilla.

Messelaar Bulb Co., Inc.
P.O. Box 269
Ipswich, MA 01938
508-356-3737
Imported Dutch bulbs such as tulip, daffodil, crocus, amaryllis, and 'Paper-white.'

Charles H. Mueller
Star Route, Box 21
New Hope, PA 18938
215-862-2033
Nearly 400 spring-, summer-, and
autumn-flowering bulbs.

Park Seed Co.
Cokesbury Road
Greenwood, SC 29647-0001
803-223-7333
A separate catalog of bulbs in
early summer offering rare bulbs,
bulbs for indoor forcing and
growing, and pre-cooled bulbs.

Quality Dutch Bulb, Inc.
P.O. Box 225
Hillsdale, NJ 07642
201-391-6586
Imported Dutch bulbs such as
amaryllis and tulip plus some
pre-cooled varieties.

John Scheepers, Inc.
Route 2, Phillipsburg Road
Middletown, NY 10940
914-342-1135
Dozens of unusual bulbs for
forcing and growing indoors with
detailed instructions: lily of the
valley, clivia, calla lily, freesia,
caladium, bulbous orchid,
gloxinia, crocus, and iris varieties.

Smith & Hawken
25 Corte Madera
Mill Valley, CA 94941
415-383-2000
Easily forced bulbs such as
amaryllis or lilies of the valley in
crates, 'Paper-whites' in baskets,
hyacinths in glass vases, and
tulips in cachepots.

Van Bourgondien Bros.
P.O. Box A
245 Farmingdale Road
Babylon, NY 11702
800-873-9444
Varieties for indoor growing
include miniature amaryllis, calla
lily and Chinese lily, which can be
ordered with containers.

Mary Mattison van Schaik
Route 1, Box 181
Cavendish, VT 05142
802-226-7338
A list of flowers for forcing,
including crocus and snowdrops.

Vandenberg
1 Black Meadow Road
P.O. Box 532
Chester, NY 10918
914-469-9161
Some pre-cooled bulbs and bulbs
for forcing with varieties of Dutch
iris, lily, tulip and crocus.

Wayside Gardens
1 Garden Lane
Hodges, SC 29695
800-845-1124
Pre-potted South American
butterfly amaryllis in wide
selection of bulbs, containers, and
garden items.

CONTAINERS

Allen, Sterling & Lothrop
191 U.S. Route 1
Falmouth, ME 04015
207-781-4142
Maine-made barrels, tubs, and
baskets.

Be Seated, Inc.
66 Greenwich Avenue
New York, NY 10011
212-924-8444
Large and changing stock of old
and new rustic baskets.

Bittersweet Farm
6294 Seville Road
Seville, OH 44273
216-887-5293
An assortment of handcrafted
products of a family farm,
including baskets adorned with
dried flowers and herbs.

Charlotte Moss
165 E. 71st Street
New York, NY 10021
212-772-6244
Antique and decorative
accessories; porcelain containers.

Gardens
1818 W. 35th Street
Austin, TX 78703
512-451-5490
Large assortment of containers in
hedge, willow, and chicken wire.
Also terra-cotta pots imported
from England.

Gardener's Eden
P.O. Box 7307
San Francisco, CA 94120-7307
415-421-4242
Portuguese terra-cotta pots,
wooden barrel planters from
England, metal flower buckets
used by the French, and bulb-
shaped vases made in the
Orient of solid brass with a
verdigris finish.

Gumps
250 Post Street
San Francisco, CA 94108-9915
800-334-8677
A supplier of traditional
porcelain planters and glass and
ceramic vases.

David Kay, Inc.
Suite 114
921 Eastwind Drive
Westerville, OH 43081
800-872-5588
Catalog of useful accessories for
the indoor garden.

Lexington Gardens
1008 Lexington Avenue
New York, NY 10021
212-861-4390
A stock of containers and baskets
of wire, split-wood, and twig.

Mrs. McGregor's Garden Shop
4801 First Street N.
Arlington, VA 22203
703-528-8773
Teak planters and garden boxes in
several different styles and sizes.

Sweetbriar Logs
507 Mt. Holyoke Avenue
Pacific Palisades, CA 90272
213-459-5647
Unusual planters made to look
like tree stumps and fallen logs
that can be used indoors.

Veen & Pol Inc.
399 Bleecker Street
New York, NY 10014
212-727-3988
An assortment of containers in
alabaster and terra-cotta, and a
selection of baskets.

Winterthur Museum & Gardens
Direct Mail Department
Winterthur, DE 19735
800-767-0500
A good variety of containers
including porcelain cachepots and
wicker and marble planters.

Wolfman-Gold & Good Company
116 Greene Street
New York, NY 10012
212-431-1888
Formal French planters and
latticework window boxes in a
selection of gardening accessories.

ACKNOWLEDGMENTS

We would like to thank all the homeowners who so generously allowed us to photograph. In particular, Bill Stites and Kathryn George want to give special thanks to:

Dan Prince
Julie and Allan Shope
Laura Kaehler
Ned and Liza Weihman
Barry and Cece Kieselstein-Cord
Sara Stites
Michael Lane
Robert Kinnaman
Brian Ramaekers

In addition, Smallwood & Stewart would like to thank Gus de Hertogh, Sally Ferguson of The Netherlands FlowerBulb Association, Cecilia Soprano and Bob Albanese, Sally Squire, Brent and Becky Heath of The Daffodil Mart; and Maggie Oster. Finally, our sincere thanks to Barbara Plumb, who had the vision to see this book and who gave us support and encouragement throughout.